Light and Shadow

William Anton

Light is all around us.

We get light from the sun.

We can get light
from electric lamps.

We can get light from flashlights.
We need light to see.

Light can shine through some things.
The sun shines through these windows.

These curtains only let
some light through.

This girl's body blocks out the light.
You can see her shadow
on the ground.

The boy and his bat
block out the light.
Can you see his shadow?

When something blocks out the light
you can see its shadow.

A shadow is dark.
A shadow has a shape.

This girl's shadow is flat.
Her shadow is flat
because the ground is flat.

This boy's shadow is not flat.
His shadow bends
because the steps bend.

Even a small thing can
have a big shadow!

How does your shadow change?